ISBN 978-0-243-38891-2
PIBN 10796511

1 MONTH OF
FREE
READING

at
www.ForgottenBooks.com

By purchasing this book you are eligible for one month membership to ForgottenBooks.com, giving you unlimited access to our entire collection of over 700,000 titles via our web site and mobile apps.

To claim your free month visit:

www.forgottenbooks.com/free796511

English
Français
Deutsche
Italiano
Español
Português

www.forgottenbooks.com

Mythology Photography **Fiction**
Fishing Christianity **Art** Cooking
Essays Buddhism Freemasonry
Medicine **Biology** Music **Ancient**
Egypt Evolution Carpentry Physics
Dance Geology **Mathematics** Fitness
Shakespeare **Folklore** Yoga Marketing
Confidence Immortality Biographies
Poetry **Psychology** Witchcraft
Electronics Chemistry History **Law**
Accounting **Philosophy** Anthropology
Alchemy Drama Quantum Mechanics
Atheism Sexual Health **Ancient History**
Entrepreneurship Languages Sport
Paleontology Needlework Islam
Metaphysics Investment Archaeology
Parenting Statistics Criminology
Motivational

INAUGURAL ADDRESS,

BY

WORTHINGTON SMITH, D. D.

. AN

INAUGURAL ADDRESS

𝔇𝔢𝔩𝔦𝔳𝔢𝔯𝔢𝔡 𝔍𝔲𝔩𝔶 31𝔰𝔱, 1849.

BY WORTHINGTON SMITH, D. D.,

President of the University of Vermont.

PUBLISHED BY THE CORPORATION.

BURLINGTON:

UNIVERSITY PRESS.

1849.

ADDRESS.

INCIDENTS like the present, though not of rare occurrence in the history of our colleges, and perhaps not of great intrinsic importance—are nevertheless permitted, through the courtesy of the Public, to occupy their hour among the events of the day.

They serve, it is conceived, as a fit occasion to invite the public mind to contemplate the uses and ends of our Literary Institutions; the wants in which they take their rise and which they are designed to supply; the abuse to which they are liable, and the neglect under which they may suffer to the public detriment; to mark their progress or decline; to observe their adaptation or unfitness to the higher developements of social life; to consider the improvements of which they are still susceptible, and the claims they may possess on the vigilance, the sympathy, and patronage of an enlightened christian public.

To a community, into which the elements of a Christian civilization were to be infused, the importance of an institution for the nurture and diffusion of sound Learning and Morals, did not escape the notice of those practical, clear-sighted men who nursed the infancy of this northern Republic. At that early period in the history of a people, when to provide for the immediate safety and sustenance of their families, to open the forest for cultivation, and defend their titles to the soil which they occupied, seem to circumscribe the duties of the citizen and the patriot; at a time when powerful adversaries beleagured them, when every man's harvest was insecure, and the future overcast with uncertainty and gloom—there were in the midst of us, and enjoying the confidence of the people because they had adopted the spirit and views of the people, a class of thoughtful, far-seeing minds who discerned in the distance a strong and healthy Republic overspreading these hills and vallies, and felt themselves called to lay its foundations in virtue and intelligence. Here was a Chittenden, a tower of confidence; a Paine, cautious, vigilant, whose high spirit disdained the craven policy of exchanging our public domain for the privilege of educating the sons of Vermont, on the soil of a sister state. Here was an Allen, of warm and generous impulses; a Chipman, sagacious, profound; a Williams, considerate, scholarlike, learned; with other worthy associates whose names will be uttered with respect in future times.

Minds of this order and of such qualities among us, were early directed to the subject of founding an university or college as a matter of high public concernment. An interval of several years indeed elapsed between the first public agitation of this subject, and the granting of a charter in 1791; yet the measure seems at no period to have been lost sight of. The idea came, in time, to pervade the general mind, that the public service rendered indispensable the aid of an educated class of men. It was perceived that for the state to deprive herself of such aid was sure to impede her growth and improvement; and to depend on foreign sources for the supply, was to sink to a provincial rank among the confederated states. It was remembered that even Rome, in the pride of her power, felt her humiliation so long as her gifted sons sought in the schools of Greece and her colonies, the nurture she had neglected to provide for them at home.

As a measure then of state economy, and for preserving state independence; and more even than this, as a means of perpetuating the character and cherishing the spirit peculiar to any people, as well as for the love of learning and the aids and incentives to its pursuit which are derived from them, no sovereign People can well dispense with the higher institutions of learning, or afford to expatriate their sons for an education. The enlightened sentiment expressed in the preamble to our charter, that " the establishment of seminaries and colleges, as they tend to render the people of any state respectable, have ever been fostered by all good governments," was fully apprehended by the early inhabitants of this state; and though few in number and far removed from a condition of affluence, they adopted measures of almost unprecedented vigor to supply within their own borders the demands for academic instruction which it was foreseen must soon arise. The poor were emulous of the rich in their individual exertions to promote so laudable an enterprise. The Legislature of the state favored it by granting a charter for an University, distinguished for its wise and liberal provisions; and set an example of public patronage by conveying to it, in perpetuity, the use of all such grants as had been made, for the benefit of a college, under the authority of the state. The public zeal thus manifested in the cause of liberal education, was not sudden-

ly extinguished. So late as the year 1810, the follow-
ing emphatic language, from the pen of Lieut. Gover-
nor Leland, was approved and adopted by the Assem-
bly, that "the interests of the University of Vermont,
originally designed to receive the immediate patronage
of the Legislature, merit the most serious and delibe-
rate consideration."

But public opinion, it must be confessed, has somewhat declined from those broad and enlightened views
on educational policy which obtained in more
primitive times; and it is even become one of the
questions of the day, and by no means confined to
weak and narrow minds, whether the time is not gone
by in which the higher institutions of Learning are to
be fostered as a distinct branch of educational economy? Do not such institutions belong to the scholastic
age of man, or to the early, formative stage of society,
and constitute one of those temporary expedients which
are useful and perhaps indispensable to the infancy of
states; but which, like certain primitive functions oc-
casionally to be met with in the animal tribes, having
fulfilled their office are superseded by other and more
perfect ones, and so at last disappear. Not only do
certain instincts, once necessary to the preservation of
life, become actually lost in the progress of the animal
towards maturity; but even the form and substance of
a vital organ is said to give place to a new developement—seeking indeed the same end, but by means of a
different apparatus, and adapting the animal to a more
etherial element and to a higher form of life. And it
may be asked, if some analogy may not be traced in
this change in the organs of animal life, to what, at a

certain period, may be expected in some of the functions of social life?

The period, in which the learned institutions of the old world are supposed to have taken their rise, is doubtless distinguishable in some essential respects from the present. Christendom was then overspread with intellectual darkness, pierced only, and at remote points, by the beams of some learned cloister, or the solitary ray of some studious hermit, struggling feebly with the all-enfolding gloom. The masses were unlettered. No method had been devised for multiplying copies of ancient or recent manuscripts to meet the demands of the few scholars of the age. The prince and the subject, the nobility and the commons, were almost alike ignorant and rude; while the sons of the Church, religious and secular, with clerkship enough to make dupes of the Laity, were withal too self-seeking and wary to betray the instruments of their power by opening inlets of knowledge to the popular mind.

Now that the few studious minds scattered over this wide intellectual waste, should be drawn together by some law of literary affinity; that masters should lead their pupils to some common point made luminous by the centralization of learned men and the helps to learning, seems to have been the only method at hand which promised the revival and diffusion of Letters. This process seems to have been historically realized in the formation of the venerable universities of Oxford and Cambridge, and not unlikely of the most early universities on the continent. Originally, as they are described to us, they were a group of independent schools under their respective masters. These in the lapse of time took on the type of permanent institutions under the denomination of colleges : and finally, by act of legislature, or what is more probable perhaps, by ·the tendency of like things to unity, these colleges, without merging their individuality, became parts of one complex institution. At such points as these, whether determined on by concert or accident, learned men would naturally be brought together ; a literary spirit would be cultivated, and literary enterprises projected. Princes and affluent men would be induced to encourage so laudable a movement by endowing faculties, and supplying expensive materials for knowledge and progress; and scholars would go forth, in time, to awaken the spirit of improvement in the mass of society. No other expedient, manifestly, could meet the wants of the social mind and supply the means of intellectual culture in such an emergency, but the fostering of a few eminent seats of Learning for the training of those who were to become the educators of the people. This, then, is the object to be sought by these institutions at the time of their rise. They were needful for the age; a remedy for the evils peculiar to the period in which they rose into being ; and it is not easy to perceive by what other expedient an impulse could have been given to the cause of improvement; or what other force, than the one here generated, could have penetrated the dormant mass of the popular mind and awakened it to intellectual life.

But gliding along a period of centuries, and especially passing from the old world where society is every where oppressed with the spirit if not the forms of feudal life, we enter an era of time and a region of the earth where a new order of social life obtains; where all is fresh and youthful, full of hope and promise.

The eye falls on a race of freemen, erect, intelligent, strong in purpose and manly in enterprise. Here progress is impeded by the accumulated wrecks of no hoary systems of folly or oppression. Here are no castes, no lords and vassals, no monopolies, or privileged orders. A bigoted Priesthood or intolerant Church, even were it so disposed, has not the power to molest our liberties or constrain our faith. Moreover, here are schools provided to nurse every new-born mind with the milk of knowledge, and train it for the duties of the man and the citizen. Here is the press, scattering over the land its pregnant sheets

" Thick as autumnal leaves that strew the brooks "
"In Vallombrosa. "

Magnificent libraries of rare and choice reading are amassed at convenient points of access, and through the liberality of their founders made available to studious youth in whatever pursuit in life. Books in almost every department of thought and inquiry, and at so moderate a price, are now exposed in our literary marts, that an ordinary farmer or mechanic is able to exhibit from his domestic shelves a more extensive and valuable collection of reading, than could often be found in learned monasteries, and even in some royal universities. Lyceums, moreover, and halls for discussion and debate, are common to the rural village as to the peopled city. Popular lectures in science and art, in history, jurisprudence, politics, and general literature, may almost every where, after a sort, be enjoyed; while instruments for scientific illustration and experiment are become familiar to our common schools. One may almost fancy himself as dwelling in the midst of a national university, where the whole people are brought together in the capacity either of master or pupil; where all aids and facilities to learning are supplied—all faculties endowed, all science and art taught; and, what is best of all, every teacher and learner domiciliated around his own hearth-stone.

Why then it is asked, and on no occasion is the question more pertinent than the present, why ought we not to dispense with these antique, scholastic, not to say, cloistered institutions? Although important and needful to society in times gone by, is not their office at length superseded—or rather absorbed in the developement of a higher, more comprehensive law of social progress, which the lapse of ages has been slowly unfolding? In short, is not their appropriate mission fulfilled; and the time come for directing the public mind to a more popular and less scholastic method for securing the higher forms of culture—while our present institutions, those venerable servitors of a past and less fortunate age, are consigned to an honorable sepulture?

In answer to inquiries of this sort, and more especially with a view to correct what is conceived to be the mistaken and narrow views whence they arise; I would ask attention, in a few remarks, to the origin, the true ground and aim, of a comprehensive system of nurture suited to a christian people; the office and influence of educational institutions. as the means of realizing the idea embodied in such a system; the place which a College must occupy in a popular educational economy, not only as an integral part thereof, but as indirectly affecting the whole; and lastly, the direct and powerful influence for good which it exerts on all the abiding interests of society.

That the educational movement of recent times took its rise in the Christian element,will be conceded by all who reflect that under a similar form Christianity put herself forth at the beginning; that she awakened a spirit of inquiry and a thirst for knowledge in whatever land she visited, however rude and barbarous; that an educational movement more or less intense, according as her power over the public mind was less or more impeded, has attended her progress through the past; and that at this day nearly the same lines which bound the area of her influence, limit also the sphere of human improvement and progress. Indeed, before a Christain audience it may be maintained, I trust, without offence, that *culture*, intellectual, moral, spiritual, social, is the proximate, definitive end which christianity proposes to itself. Its Founder is denominated 'a Teacher come from God'—'the Light of the world'—He himself utters the emphatic words before the Roman prefect—"to this end was I born, and for this cause came I into the world that I should bear witness unto the truth." This was the boon which an ignorant, miserable race needed, and which it sighed for from the Father of lights—'the God of all grace.'

There was no lack of devotion on the earth—devotion earnest and absorbing; but uninformed, misapplied, and therefore degrading. There were 'lords many and gods many.' Temples, exhausting the wealth and artistic skill of nations, adorned the cities of men. Altars smoked from the high places of the earth, and idols smiled or frowned on all places of concourse for business or pleasure. What was needed was a teacher, a witness to the truth—an informing, guiding, hallowing power to restore a lapsed race, and gather the dispersed into the kingdom of God. A mission for such ends Divine Wisdom vouchsafed in the person of a Mediator; and from that moment a new system of teaching and culture, adequate to the wants of an immortal mind, and suited to the manifold conditions of the race, dawned upon the world. A religion that wrought inwardly that it might work outwardly; a religion of ideas, principles, sentiments, and not merely of forms or impulses, became the inheritance of man. The Teacher henceforth took the place of the Priest; and thought, living and imperishable, began to awaken and direct the activities of dormant intellect.

The Church, as the embodiment of christianity, is essentially a school for learning and nurture. This is one of the marks by which in all times and places she has been identified—her *quod ubique, quod semper, et quod ab omnibus.* It is this feature that distinguishes christianity from all other known religions, and gives her pre-eminence over all. Other religions may have tolerated intellectual developement; or to speak more truly, may not have been able to arrest it. It is the Christian that aids, quickens, and directs this developement; inviting to the utmost expansion of intellectual and moral power, and teaching it to invade all fields of thought and knowledge, and enterprise.

The Church is christianity under its outward, social aspect; representing historically its true tendencies, and to be regarded as the exponent of its power for any particular place or age. This element from above leavens the mass which it permeates, and becomes to society, what it is in its own nature, 'The truth and the Life.' It influences the spirit, the customs and general character of society, by influencing the individuals of which society is composed. Adapting itself to man's higher nature, and becoming to him a'life within life, it awakens the intellect to all earnest thought, and the heart to insatiable longings and strivings after the stature of the full-grown man. As a philosophical, no less than popular description of the social influences of christianity, our mother tongue does not supply a more significant term than that of 'Awakening'—a word hallowed by the usage of more serious and devout times; but now alike abused both by cant and ribaldry. Whatever christianity does for the individual or the mass, it does by an influence which this word imports. It is a spirit giving life—quickening the latent powers and sensibilities of the mind, and supplying at once the impulse and the law of its progress.

It is then in the Christian element that we seek the ground-form, the scope, and aim of a system of education suited to a Christian people. Historically, christianity is the condition on which a system of popular education is possible. Such a system can be realized only as it is a part of christianity itself—taking its type and model, as well as its inception and impulse from this supernatural element. By means of popular nurture it is, that christianity strives for its highest realization on the earth; and only as a people are actually or prospectively Christian, are they competent to receive the benefit of such a system of nurture. She embodies herself no less truly in an educational than in an ecclesiastical Polity. Her home is the school-house and the college no less than the sanctuary; her servants, the teachers of our youth, as well as the ministers in high places. Hostility to popular education, to the established means and methods for its promotion, no less than hostility to the Church and her institutions, is war against christianity, and war penetrating to her firesides and altars.

As then christianity is the source of our educational movement, so we seek her guidance in the systems we construct and in the aims we pursue. We adopt a system for the whole community; because christianity eschews distinction between Jew and Greek, the bond and free; and society must repudiate its christianity when it proposes to leave any order or condition of mind without the means of culture. Moreover, we aim to impart knowledge to the open and susceptible mind; not however for the alone sake of knowledge, but primarily as the means of developement and train-ing—the material for thought to work upon, and by working to give strength, and aptitude, and self-control to the mind, that it may grow up to the stature, the power, and symmetry of the perfect man. And here it will occur to the merely casual observer, that knowl-edge, as existing objectively and in formulas or facts, subserves a two-fold purpose; as an instrument of the mind's self-nurture, and as an auxiliary to its power when applied to the concerns of life. A limited amount of information may suffice for the first purpose, provided it be of such diversity as to elicit the manifold capabilities of the mind; while for the other, no extent or variety of intellectual wealth will be found superflu-ous. For the end here proposed, let the decree go forth, ' that all the world should be taxed.' Contem-plating mind under a mere intellectual aspect, the prop-er aim of education is, as we conceive, to impart to it aptitude, comprehension, power. Dogmatic teaching, or a knowledge of formulas and facts, are mainly useful as they stimulate the susceptibilities of the mind, supply occasions for the developement and exercise of its powers, and form it to just methods of thought, as well as to the needful habits of patience and self-reliance. When this end is accomplished, then comes the period for accumulation—for enlarging and arranging its intellectual stores.

But, again, a Christian system of education is not realized in the developement and training of the intellectual faculties alone. It is not a race of giants which it proposes to rear—prodigies of mere intellectual stature and strength; but minds endued with the spirit and virtues of Christian men, qualified for the offices of private life, and fitted to adorn the various stations to be occupied in a Christian commonwealth. The spirit of a people, their conscience, their moral and social sensibilities, their opinions, customs, habits, need to be nurtured and directed, no less than those mental powers on which the acquisition of knowledge depends. This must enter into the aim of all educational enterprises that claim to be Christian; and moreover such results must in a measure be realized, or a Christian people will repudiate such enterprises as unsuited to their aim and destination; and the schools and colleges of the land will become deserted and left to die.

Having thus far taken a general survey of that system of mental and moral culture which is suited to the youth of a Christian state; it becomes natural to inquire for the means and processes of realizing the end proposed. And here we may do well to ask, is there a self-educating method, so simple, so attractive, so commensurate to the needs of the mind and the duties of life, as to be actually available to the common mass of

society? Is it in the order of human events, that each
generation in any community grows up to full intellectual power and expansion,as the body, by natural caus-
es and in a given period of years, attains to the stature
and strength of the perfect man? Will community
rise to this state by such precarious and fitful aids, as
they will be likely to derive from those of elder growth
and cultivation than themselves? Moreover, should
knowledge be diffused in most ample measures, by
means of books and the periodical press, would even
this supply the absence of set forms and long continued
processes for instructing and training the youthful mind
of the people? Do such appliances, where the most
concentrated, avail in raising to a high intellectual
state the lower masses that congregate in our cities?
In short, is not man in all the phases of developement
of which his inner being is susceptible, the creature of
Institutions—uncultivated and savage in their absence,
but civilized and elevated according to the perfection
to which these attain, and to the force with which they
act on the people? Nay more, what is the social state
itself—the only state in which man can truly become
man, and in which improvement, beyond the sphere of
mere instinct or of absolute necessity, is hardly con-
ceivable—but a state of institutions, acknowledged, re-
spected, depended on for the well-being of those who
live under them? These are not only the manifesta-
tions of the social life already begun, the exponents of
its maturity and power; but the organs of its future
growth and perpetuity. They are institutions that
create a people; and hence God ordained them for
man at a period, when man was untaught to provide
them for himself. Time, with the aid of experience or

accident, may modify the forms of our institutions; but the things themselves must remain, or man takes a retrograde direction and society itself hastens to dissolution.

Institutions of Law and Religion exist wherever the relation of man to man, or of man to his Creator is recognized. The one forms the natural basis of human government, the other, the necessary condition to the being of a church—the one controlling men for the purposes of society, the other nurturing them for the kingdom of heaven. Institutions of Learning, which are of later origin but which are to be found in a less or more complete state, wherever civilization and christianity obtain—may be regarded as those organic contrivances by which a people seek to supply their intellectual wants, and aid their advancement to a higher and more perfect state. What community would think of dispensing with its religious institutions—its church, its Sabbath, its public assemblies, its teaching ministry—but as preparatory to dispensing with religion itself? What people would think of repudiating their Common Schools and depending in future on the silent teachings of the press, who had not first concerted to extinguish the light of knowledge before the eyes of their children, and bring back Cimmerian darkness and the reign of old Night upon their land?

Colleges or Universities—so styled because they take a wider scope than schools of a lower grade, and are adapted to a higher sphere of instruction and discipline—are but one in a series of institutions which together form the educational polity of a cultivated people. As institutions they are organic parts of the body politic—essential, if not to its being, at least to its well-being; and for the reason that they concern themselves with the more advanced stage of mental culture, they serve as the support, the regulator of the whole system of popular education—as, historically and by the order of necessity, they were the first in the series.

That these institutions are public, precisely in the sense that common schools are public—contemplating a direct influence on all the indiviual minds that shall in time constitute the public—it is not needful to affirm. There are many things from which important benefits accrue to the public, which at the same time are not common to the individuals of that public, as the roadside or the light of heaven are common. We do maintain, however, that colleges are public and common in the highest sense which the people of a state choose to have them. They are created for high public purposes; they have a specific, ultimate aim to the public weal; they are accessible to all the sons of the state, whom a love of learning, or a desire for distinction and usefulness may prompt to a course of liberal study: and that they are not even free to such and free to all, is due to their narrow endowments rather than to any exclusive spirit of which they may be accused. The end which they propose to themselves is human culture in its largest sense: If not directly to advance sound learning at its fountain head, at least to select and arrange, to diffuse and render available to society at large, the labors of studious minds; to foster the spirit of learning, and train the youth committed to their care to 'serve their generation by the will of God'—Faithless to its true purpose and aim is that school of learning which sinks itself to the level of a trade—working merely for its own ends, or limiting its offices to a certain mercenary influence on the few minds that are attracted to its halls.

A worthy and noble end is doubtless achieved when even a few youthful minds are imbued with the true spirit of liberal study, inured to patient and scholarlike habits of thought, and enriched with various stores of knowledge.

But even in no such result as this, is the design of a truly liberal institiution fully realized. It has a wider scope—a far loftier aim. She seeks indeed, as a proximate end, to nurture the individual mind; but she ever more looks forward to the day when her sons shall go forth to strengthen and adorn the social fabric. She allies herself to all the great and abiding interests of the community, in whose bosom she herself is fostered. She regards herself and those who are nurtured at her fountains of truth and knowledge, as the humble servitors of the Church and State. So far as she enjoys the patronage of the public, and within her appropriate sphere, she charges herself with seeing that the public service is provided for. She would supply the schools of the land with competent teachers, or otherwise aid in elevating that branch of useful labor to the demands of the age. Her aim is to prepare strong and earnest men for the Pulpit; and to endue with science and skill those who are destined to the liberal or industrial Arts of life. She aspires to the honor of rearing statesmen for the Cabinet, jurists for the Bench, orators for the Forum and the Senate, and safe and powerful thinkers for the Press.

And can an enlightened, progressive community with safety to her true interests, dispense with institutions of such aims—that have been and that still are productive

in such results? Have the people of this land reached
that point, at which they may begin to depend on other means and appliances for supplying the public service either in Church or State? Nay, is not the main
argument against the fostering of these institutions, the
very one, on which their utility and necessity may be
urged with complete success before an intelligent and
candid tribunal? In the same proportion that the
standard of intelligence rises among the people, must
we add to the stature aud strength of those minds
which are to influence and guide the people. The
men of power in one age, are not the men of power
for all ages; they must rise with the people whom they
assume to lead; or the people will tread them down in
their might, or kindly pass them back upon the age to
which they belong. Conceding the fact, as we are hap-
py to do, that the means of knowledge are far more
amply and widely supplied to our people than at any
former period in our history, or in the history of man—
that far more intelligence is actually diffused, and that
men were never so competent to think and speculate
wisely for themselves; the only use that can be made
of this concession, to the case in hand, is to make more
obvious the necessity for the higher institutions of learning as the means of providing that order of intelligence
and culture suited to the wants of the age. How shall
the Pulpit, or the Bench, or the Hall of legislation, or
the periodical Press, continue to be held in respect and
to sway their accustomed influence over the public
mind, unless they be served with a power of intelligence and thought, that shall preserve itself in advance
of the people? There remains but this alternative—
the masses must be arrested in their progress, or minds

of high intellectual culture and power called into service. We conclude, then, that it is no time to decry the
higher institutions of Learning, when even the industrial classes among us are solving deeper problems and
supplying themselves with a higher order of literature
than even the majority of educated men were masters
of fifty years ago; that if colleges are ever indispensable to a people, it is not when at their lower, but at
their higher stage of culture. In a community advanced and advancing like our own, the *present* would
be the epoch for such institutions to appear, if they had
not already appeared; and the question in regard to
them, most likely to interest liberal and thinking minds
would not be, whether they should cease? but how
shall they be made more commensurate to the wants
of this and coming times?

The very great number to which the Literary institutions among us, professedly of the higher class, have
attained—as it betrays a tendency to excess—may
have contributed to bring the system itself into disre-
pute. An European might naturally ask himself, what
necessity for a hundred and twenty colleges, can there
be among a people whose aggregate population does
not exceed twenty millions? Or, by what rule of political economy do they find their interest in supporting
so expensive an establishment for the education of only
ten thousand young men? Why not consolidate them
into a small number, and thereby enlarge their endowments to the standard of the institutions of the Old
World?

The fact here adverted to is doubtless felt to be an
evil at home as well as abroad. But in passing on the
wisdom or folly of this arrangement, it is but just to

consider the extent of our domain in comparison to the circumscribed spaces occupied by the several states of Europe; and, in the second place, the genius and policy of our people as exhibited in almost all their social arrangements. The argument for greatly reducing the number of our colleges, would cut deep at the same time into the very fabric of our political organization. *Thirty* distinct governments, duly appointed for a state of peace or war, and yet in important respects limited and controlled by a superior and all-embracing legislation—might seem an awkward and lavish contrivance for protecting the rights of men. But in these and kindred matters, the question is not—what is the simplest and the cheapest; but what sorts best with the genius and habits of the people? Our political arragements may neither be wise or economical in the judgment of others; but they serve at least, to gratify a humor we have; and what is more, to secure, as we conceive,some substantial benefits for which we can afford to be taxed.

For a like reason a democratic and widely spread people must be indulged in some peculiarities in regard to their Literary institutions. Our national, cherished policy is thoroughly adverse to all *centralizing* tendencies. We are jealous of the great accumulation of political, commercial, and monetary power; we choose to have it diffused over the broad domain, even at the risk of a great reduction. We betray the same spirit, at least, we adopt the same policy in regard to the higher institutions of learning. If they are a local as well as public benefit; or if their utility is to be measured by the numbers they educate, rather than by the degree of culture they impart to a comparatively few, then let them multiply with the people to enjoy them. The voice of the people is, Let these lights be distributed throughout the great house of the nation even though they may burn with a feebler radiance; rather than condensed into one brilliant, intense, central blaze, leaving the extreme parts shaded in 'disastrous twilight.' Such is the policy that prevails among us; and the wise men of this day will leave it undisturbed; and only strive to make it the most conducive to the public good.

But from the train of thought into which I have been led by the seeming demands of the occasion, I return for a moment to our own institution and to the incident which occasions the present ceremony. The University of Vermont was created for the purpose of realizing that idea of a liberal education which was early entertained by the leading minds in our state. Its appellation may indeed sound somewhat lofty and ambitious on prudish ears; and as a mere matter of taste a more modest style ,perhaps, might have become the lips of a democratic people. Still, if we regard the name only as significant of the intention of its founders—to make it the one, the universal college for the state—the objection loses much of its force. It was deemed important that Vermont should be supplied with a College adequate to its wants, and felt to be desirable that it should enjoy the united patronage of the state; and hence it received its present designation. The *location* of the college was the result of slow and cautious deliberation; and its present site was determined on, it would seem, by its relation to other institutions of the same rank, and by a prospective regard to the future population of the state, and to those local, physical advantages which must always influence the industrial and mercantile enterprises of a people. And who that surveys the area of our state—or the population and wealth that have accumulated and are still accumulating in our northern sections, and the points toward which business and trade are tending; or who glances his eye over the range of prospect, or studies the grand and picturesque scenery that environs its present site—will call in question the wisdom of that decision? Other plans and those of sectional origin and aim, subseqently arose to disturb the scheme at first entertained; but though it will be the subject of regret that the counsels of the friends of education among us became thus divided, let it now be the concern of all to render this evil as inoperative as possible.

Embarrassments and disasters not uncommon to new institutions in a new country, have attended the rise and history of this University; yet its course has been onward, until it has reached a point in respectability and usefulness unsurpassed, we must think, by any institution within the same period of its growth. But the college, like the state that fosters it, is still in its youth.—It feels, we trust, the impulses, cherishes the strivings, and is stimulated by the hopes which belong to the youth of life. It is her ambition by her labors and results—by the tone of scholarship, of manly virtue, and Christian piety, which she may nurture here; and by the intelligence and power, the devoted, earnest spirit she may contribute to the service of the Church and State—to deserve well of the people who have called her into being. She hopes to enjoy the counsels of the wise, the benedictions of the good, the approbation of all. She desires to make her retreats safe and attractive to the youth of the state; and by the number and the qualifications of those who go forth from her, She would aspire to the highest honor that is reserved to human agency.—that of serving the generations of men according to the will of God. Her expectation is to grow with the growth of the people—to be strengthened with their strength; and to feel the weight and infirmities of years, only when the strong pillars of society itself shall give signs of weariness and decay!

I may already have trespassed on the patience of my audience; but a just regard to my own feelings as well as to the proprieties of the occasion, is my apology for detaining you by a few remarks to *the present members of College.*

In presenting myself before you at this time, young Gentlemen, it is pleasant to reflect that I may do it, if not as a personal acquaintance, at least as one who may make some pretensions to a special interest in your welfare. I come to you from among the same people in whose bosom most of you were born and nurtured. I have mingled with them in the toils and assiduities of life. I have studied their character; I have adopted their customs; I have become imbued with their spirit. Their interests and mine have long since become one. For twenty-five years past my duties have often called me to the college; I have borne an humble part in her counsels; I have participated in her anxieties and encouragements, and cherished an interest in the success of those who have resorted hither for instruction. May I not then offer myself to you as an acquaintance and friend; may I not ask it of you to receive me with that open and confiding spirit which shall assure me that I am still at home.

I come hither, young men, not in pursuit of honors or

to enjoy repose; but to seek your welfare, and to aid in preparing you for honor and usefulness among men. It shall be my endeavor to assist you with such counsels as my wisdom and experience may supply; to guard you from such dangers as beset the path of the youthful mind; to soothe your anxieties; to make your toils pleasant; and by all proper incitements encourage you to the pursuit of whatsoever things are true, and lovely, and of good report. Yea, in the awful language of scripture, I will charge myself 'to watch for your souls as one that must give account!'

Be it your concern, young Friends, to reciprocate such aims and good offices from me and my associates, by a courteous and manly deportment—by diligent application to your several duties—by a ready and cheerful observance of the order and discipline of college—and a manifested desire to make our labors pleasant though arduous. Then will our acquaintance soon ripen into a friendship that will survive the short period of our college connexion, and be renewed, we may hope, in that 'life beyond life,' to which God grant we may all aspire!

CPSIA information can be obtained
at www.ICGtesting.com
Printed in the USA
LVHW021248071118
596294LV00004B/703